DE LA NUIT
ORACLE

ALEXANDRA V. BACH
CAROLE - ANNE ESCHENAZI

LO SCARABEO

DE LA NUIT
ORACLE

A deck by
Carole-Anne Eschenazi and Alexandra V. Bach

Artwork by Alexandra V. Bach
Texts by Carole-Anne Eschenazi

Editing by Elena Delmastro and Riccardo Minetti
Graphic and Layout by Chiara Demagistris
Translations by Studio RGE

Printed by Wai Man Book Binding China Ltd.
Printed in July 2021

Lo Scarabeo
Via Cigna 110
10155 Torino – Italy
info@loscarabeo.com
www.loscarabeo.com

Follow **Lo Scarabeo Tarot**
on Facebook and Instagram

TABLE OF CONTENTS

English
5

Italiano
43

Español
69

Português
95

DE LA NUIT
ORACLE

ONCE UPON A TIME

Once upon a time, there was a duet made of two French artists. One was the gifted illustrator Alexandra V. Bach, who was famous for creating romantic, gorgeous, and inspiring artworks. The other was the Tarot expert and author Carole-Anne Eschenazi. Together, they had previously paired to conceive the *Tarot de la Nuit* deck. After revisiting the world of the Waite-Smith Tarot, the duet decided to go further and explore the magical world of traditional fairytales. Carole-Anne chose among the most beloved characters of worldwide known tales and selected 30 of them. Then, she wrote about their hidden meanings and symbols, while Alexandra recreated their whole universe through her artistic vision. Their goal was really to propose something new, to reinvent the images that we all associate with the classical tales. And it was also about the "Night"; about this dark yet beautiful universe, already shown in the *Tarot de la Nuit*, in which Carole-Anne and Alexandra wanted the fairytales-taken-from characters to bathe in. This is how the *De la Nuit Oracle* was born.

In the booklet, you will find for each card a brief summary of the character's story and the message this character has to deliver.

We really hope that the journey you're about to begin with the cards will be magical, enchanted and inspiring. This is our deepest wish. Reconnect to your inner child, open yourself to the beauty of fundamental stories, let your imagination take control. May Cinderella, Snow-White, Sleeping Beauty, Peter Pan, Mary Poppins, Rapunzel and all their folks, accompany you from day to day. And may they guide you on the road to *Happily ever after*…

HOW TO USE THIS DECK

Before you start using your deck on a regular basis, we strongly suggest that you do a few rituals in order to create a true bond with it.

Ritual 1: what is your favorite fairytale? Once you've determined what is your most cherished tale, check into the booklet the meaning of this story and see what information this meaning can give you about yourself.

Ritual 2: flip through the cards and determine which image appeals you the most and which the least. Check into the booklet the meanings of those two cards, and see what information this may give about your present state. (You can repeat this ritual from time to time: you will notice that your preferences are likely to vary.)

Ritual 3: before doing any personal reading with a personal question, start by questioning your deck in a more general way. For instance, ask: "Dear deck, welcome into my life, please tell me what is your first message to me?"

Also you may want to buy a special notebook in which you will write the results of all your readings with the *De la Nuit Oracle*.

ONE CARD READINGS

– *Message of the day*: ask your deck: "What message or lesson do I need to learn today?"

– *Guide of the day*: ask your deck: "Which fairytale hero should be my inspirational guide today?"

– *Question of the day*: if you have a special question concerning a personal matter, ask your deck to give you answers about it. If you feel you need more than one card to get a correct answer, feel free to pick up several cards. If you have several questions, you can ask them successively and pick up as many cards to get an answer for each one of them.

– *Meditation of the day*: if you're accustomed to meditate, you can use the cards as a tool of meditation. Ask a question, pick up a card, and imagine that you're "entering" the tale. Then take a moment to imagine what advises or answers the character would give you.

THE FAIRYTALE DE LA NUIT SPREAD

Here is the special spread specifically designed for this deck. Pick up seven cards than place them as follows:

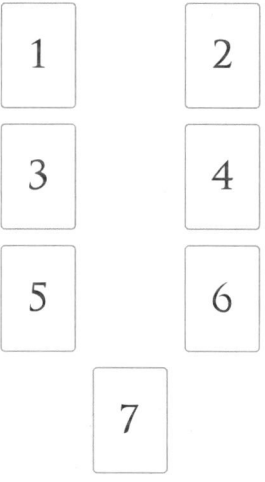

Once all the cards have been placed into the seven positions, use the booklet to find the meanings of each.

1 – The once upon a time card: it represents the very beginning of your quest, the place you're starting from.

2 – The weakness card: it represents your flaws or the places where you may be vulnerable.

3 – The initiation card: it represents the journey you're about to embark on, the adventure you have to live in order to grow.

4 – The gift card: it represents your allies, your blessings, what is given to you, your inner strengths.

5 – The magic card: it represents what you must do in order to pour some magic back into your life.

6 – The great lesson card: it represents the lesson you have to learn at this point in your life through this whole journey.

7 – The Happily ever after card: it represents what is needed now so that things can work out for the best.

There are no rigid rules and if you feel like it, you can also create your own readings. Always let your intuition and inspiration guide you.

1 · SPIRIT OF MAGIC

My story: I believe in fairies, I believe in tales, I believe in magic. I just have to open my little magical music box and the Spirit of Magic floats all around me. I pay no attention to those who try to convince me that magic is childish and that believing is a waste of time. I have been raised in the Spirit of Magic, and I know that this is the source of everything on this sweet planet. I will never stop seeing magic everywhere, nor will I stop believing.

My message: Do you believe in fairies? Do you believe in tales? Do you believe in magic? You do: bravo! You don't: you should! Anyway, you have to open yourself to the great Spirit of Magic. That means being able to see everything as a true miracle, and believing that a powerful magic surrounds you, helping you manifesting your highest dreams. Connect to the Spirit of Magic, and Magic will abound in your life.

My story: I saw once a white rabbit running on the grass. As I'm a curious little girl, I followed him. And this led me to discover a land like no other, full of mad hatters, short-tempered queens and sly cats. Everything there was purely senseless, but I saw lot of wonders, and learned many things. Therefore the journey was worth it, even if it was maybe only a dream.

My message: Something or someone is calling you. You're about to discover a brand new land, which you'll have to acclimatize to. You won't get all the rules at once. Some things will appear most peculiar to your eyes and even lacking sense. And you also will feel disoriented at times. But don't let that stop you. Be open, be curious. Crave to uncover wonders. And remember that this journey you're embarking on is really worth the while. It is really one that you won't forget.

My story: I used to live with my wicked stepmother and her vain and selfish daughters. Still I kept my faith and hope unharmed. Then one day, the king planned a ball at the castle, to get his son the prince choosing a wife. This is when my fairy godmother appeared and offered me a dress, a carriage and glass slippers. After many adventures, I eventually got to marry my sweet prince and be happy at last.

My message: Obstacles are on your way? Do not let them discourage you or demoralize you. Do not lose yourself in bitterness. Keep your faith strong, keep your hope alive. And also, keep a kind and generous heart. Your dreams will prove to be right in the end. They will come true. And you will get some kind of magical help, in the most unexpected way. In the meantime, just dig in and wait for the big moment, near to come, where you will rise and shine.

My story: I had this jealous stepmother. She couldn't stand the idea of me being more beautiful than she was. She sent a hunter to kill me. I found refuge in the forest, inside the house of seven adorable dwarfs. The queen, disguised as an old lady, tried to kill me again, with a poisoned apple. I fell in a deadly sleep. Angry and sad, the dwarfs killed the queen. And a charming prince saved me with a true love kiss, and took me to his castle.

My message: There may be jealous and mean people around you. But please don't let them poison your heart. Kindness is a most precious thing that always wins in the end. Even when scared or sad, don't stop being kind. Kindness will always make you beautiful and lovable. Sweetness and softness can really do no harm in this cruel world. So raise my flag high my dear, and be as kind as you can.

5 · SLEEPING BEAUTY

My story: Being a princess, my life was supposed to be only sweet and joyful. Alas, a cruel witch casted a spell upon me. She predicted that one day, I would prick my finger on a spinning wheel's spindle and die. And this is what almost happened. Fortunately, a good fairy partially reversed the curse: instead of dying, I only fell into a profound sleep. From which I emerged some time later by the true love's kiss of a handsome prince.

My message: The time has come to be very patient and, most importantly, to rest. You have exhausted yourself lately, having to face bad witches and curses. So your body badly needs a holiday. Don't fight against the current. Break away from your everyday life. Take the time to sleep well, think calmly and rejuvenate. Things will work out fine once you come back from this little time off.

My story: I was on my way to visit my grandmother when I met this wolf. I didn't realize how dangerous he was nor how hungry. Thoughtlessly I spoke to him and, even worse, I showed him the way to granny's home. He ran to her house, ate her, and took her place in bed. When I arrived I noticed that something was strange but I stayed just the same. Some say that, in the end, the wolf ate me. Some others say that a hunter saved me. Anyway this was a lesson to remember.

My message: Beware, there is great danger around the corner! If you have to go through the woods, do not leave the path! Be very careful about what you do and what you say. Don't trust people too lightly. Be cautious, be on your guard. A wolf is eager to eat you. So the best thing to do right now is just to keep yourself out of his way and not leave the path that will lead you home safe and sound.

My story: I am a very special witch, mostly known and feared in Russia. I live in this strange and frightful little house that you see. I have great power over the animals of the forest. And, this I must confess, I also love human flesh as a treat, most especially when it is children's flesh. Those who meet me will never forget this encounter.

My message: A time of great and powerful initiation has come for you. You are in the middle of a dark and creepy forest, standing at the doorstep of a strange house, where lives an even more strange and scary creature. Your courage is going to be put to the test. You will experiment tears, doubt and fear, that is for sure. But you will also learn a great deal about yourself, discovering your deepest strength and inner truths. It won't always be easy, but in the end, it will make you grow.

My story: I married this wealthy and powerful man without knowing the nightmare I would endure. There was this room in the castle he had forbidden me to step into. But one day I opened the door with the golden key, and found out the bloody murdered corpses of my husband's former wives. He threatened me badly for my behavior. Fortunately, my sister Anne and my brothers came to my rescue and killed Bluebeard. And we all enjoyed his fortune from this day on.

My message: Be careful, be careful, and be careful once more. Something is quite unhealthy in here, and a deep dark secret is hidden somewhere. Watch every step you make, be cautious, be warned. Don't be fooled by a golden appearance. Your opponent is sly and cruel. Go find the truth. It probably won't be very pretty. But you have to face it at last. Then gather your allies around you to help you overcome this enemy.

My story: I am the fairest of them all. Or at least I used to be. Lately my magic mirror had the nerve to tell me that my stepdaughter Snow-White is even fairer than me, which led me to some jealous rage, as you can imagine. I cannot let anyone dethrone me. So right now I'm evolving a diabolical plan, including dark forests, cruel hunters and poisoned apples. And we'll see who's the fairest in the end!

My message: I can feel jealousy, rivalry and unhealthy competition here. And believe me, I know what I'm talking about. Are you the jealous one? Or are you surrounded by envious people? In both cases, be very cautious. A heart that is filled with jealousy can play many evil little tricks that lead to chaos and destruction. So if you want calm and freedom of mind, keep out of this meaningless rivalry. By doing so you'll be the smartest of them all.

My story: I exchanged the only cow my mother and I owned for a handful of magical beans. Mother was very angry and sent me to bed without dinner. Feeling quite ashamed, I threw the bloody beans through my window. Next morning, there was this huge beanstalk in my garden. I climbed it high in the sky and reach a strange land, where I found a castle in which lived a mean and rich giant. I managed to kill him and steal his golden treasure so that mother and I could live happy and well from this day on.

My message: You have to be dauntless, you have to be intrepid. Maybe you've made some mistakes recently, but the past is past. For now, you have to climb up the big beanstalk and discover some new land where you can meet luck, fame and fortune. There will be giants to fight in the process for sure. But you're cunning enough to overcome them. So go Jack, go!

11 · VASSILISSA THE BEAUTIFUL

My story: My cruel stepmother sent me to Baba Yaga's hut to get some fire. Luckily, I carried my magical doll with me. The witch asked me to perform some domestic tasks for her to earn my fire. My doll helped me. After a while, Baba Yaga sent me home, with a skull-lantern, full of burning coals. Once at home, the coals burned my stepmother and stepsisters. I ended up marrying a tsar and living happily with my husband, father and doll.

My message: You are going to need courage and bravery because some hard times are coming. You will have to accomplish very demanding tasks. Yet don't be frightened. You will be helped all along the way. And through patience and perseverance, you will find your way home. Keep going, don't lose hope. In the end, your enemies will be neutralized, and you will get to start a new and happy chapter of your life.

Our story: When the famine settled over the kingdom, our parents decided to leave us into the woods. After wandering in the forest for a long time, we finally came upon a very peculiar house, made of gingerbread. There lived a witch who trapped us and fed us so we could get fat enough to become a good meal for her. One day, we managed to throw her in the oven, and we put our hands on her treasures, that we brought home.

Our message: Cleverness and solidarity are required. You have to be smart and cunning for you're in the middle of a tricky situation. But you also have to rely on others, for you'll need all the support you can get. Union is the key. Four hands are better than two, two brains are better than one. Being *not* alone can be your strength on this matter. So find your right partner and, together, throw the ugly witches away.

My story: I appear in almost every tale. I am whether a curse or a revenge being thrown into the hero's path. I belong to the night, the fog, and cauldron's smokes. I am feared. And quite rightfully. For I bring hard times along the way. Yet always comes the time where I come to an end. I cannot be eternal. I am only here to test the will and courage of those whose souls I'm being cast upon. And the lessons – and sometimes rewards – offered once I'm done are invaluable.

My message: First, you must be very careful whom you give your trust to these days. People are not that much well-intentioned around you right now. Second, you must accept the fact that you're entering into some unpleasant moment where everything will seem to go the wrong way. No curse here though. Just a few obstacles that need to be shut down. Gather your strength and reason, and make your way through the fog.

My story: There was a prince, who only wanted to marry a true princess, with royal manners. I showed up at his castle on a stormy night. The prince's mother decided to test me. She placed a pea in my bed, under twenty mattresses. In the morning, my back hurt badly because of this pea. This sensitivity proved the prince that I was a true princess. So we married. And the pea was placed in a museum!

My message: Do what my prince did and never go for second best. Only the *very* best is to be searched for. Don't apologize for being demanding. Don't let them convince you that your wish is impossible and won't happen. You know exactly what you want, and you know exactly why and how. So be it. Sometime soon, the exact thing you're looking for will appear, as perfect as hoped for. And it will win all the tests handily. So keep asking for the best.

15 · THE PRINCESS AND THE FROG

My story: I am a princess. One day, as I was playing in the royal garden with my gold ball, it dropped into a pond. A strange frog appeared and proposed to retrieve the ball, under the condition that I accept to marry him. I accepted, too carelessly. That night, the frog showed up at the palace. My father lectured me and forced me to keep my word. Alone in the bedroom with the frog, I was so disgusted that I threw him against the wall. He then turned into a charming prince.

My message: You have made a promise, you have given your word. Maybe too hastily, too carelessly. Anyway you must meet your commitment. You cannot weasel out from your responsibilities. Of course, the situation seems to have very bad sides, that you don't want to cope with. However, maybe there is a hidden gift in here. But you will only find it by being true to your commitment.

My story: I live in Neverland, with my little fairy Tinker Bell and the lost boys. My fiercest enemy is captain Hook. From time to time, I fly to London to pick up my dear friend Wendy and her brothers. Some fairy dust, a few happy thoughts, and they all can fly with me, and get to live extraordinary adventures in Neverland. We have so much fun in here, far away from the adult world. That's why I will never grow up. This I swear!

My message: Your inner child is calling you, and wants you to have some fun. Forget about the grey and boring world of grown-ups. Only just for a while. There is a whole Neverland to be rediscovered within you. Let go of your responsibilities. Reconnect to your youthful joy. Remember that happy thoughts can truly make you fly. What are your happy thoughts? And what is your inner child begging you to do right now?

My story: I loved him so much, he was so handsome. I saved him from drowning. But he was a human prince and I was a mermaid living under the waters. Such an impossible love. So, I went to see the Sea Witch, and made a dangerous bargain with her. I gained human though hurtful legs. Alas the prince chose another woman. My heart broke for I sacrificed and endured so much for this man. In despair, I chose death and went to Heaven, at last.

My message: Something is not very healthy and very fair in here. It seems that you're the one making all the efforts. You're swimming into troubled waters. Beware dishonest bargains. You have high hopes and pure love. But a love that leads you to hurt and sacrifice yourself is not True Love. The same applies for any kind of relationship or circumstance. Save yourself from this dead-end story and go find some brighter sea elsewhere.

My story: A wicked witch had locked me away in a tower, using my long hair to climb up to me. One day, a prince discovered the tower. He climbed up and we fell in love. But the witch found out about our hopes of marriage. In anger, she cut off my hair and scratched my poor prince's eyes. We were separated for years. But then one day, after wandering through the country for years, the prince found me in the wilderness. From this moment on, we lived happily together.

My message: You have locked yourself in an ivory tower, which in a way is fine since by doing so you have learned to grow self-sufficient. However, the moment has come for you to get out of this protective yet limited cocoon. Time is running quick. You cannot spend your whole life away from the world. So carefully choose who you let *in* and, even more important, choose to get *out* and free yourself from everything that could restrain your territory.

My story: The war was raging in the whole country. And my father was old and tired. I couldn't let him go to the front. So I disguised myself as a man and went to his place. I fought courageously, taking great care that no one would find out about my true identity. I was helped by a guardian dragon. The most important thing for me was to defend the honor of my name and family, whatever the perils.

My message: Your honor is engaged. Maybe you were not the one supposed to get involved in this war. But now your solidarity dictates you to take part in the fight. You're going to need a lot of strength and bravery, for the battle will be quite rough. And you will certainly have to go under cover. But in the end, you will succeed, your folks will be very proud of you, and you will discover resources within you that you didn't even know existed.

My story: I was boring in my lonesome castle. So one day, I kidnapped a boy, who had been wounded by pieces of a magical broken mirror, and could not have feelings anymore. But there was this little girl friend of his. She overcame many perilous adventures to find her friend. When she arrived in my castle, Kay did not recognize her at all, for his heart was frozen. Gerda cried, and her tears warmed Kay's heart. They left my palace and I was left alone once again.

My message: You're in such a state of isolation, this is not healthy. It has to stop. You have to get out of your frozen castle, you have to make some new friends, you have to learn how to warm your world. You have been experimenting loneliness and autarky for long enough. Spring has to come again. You need some sun, you need flowers, you need green trees. So put an end to your own winter, and go create some new joyful bonds.

My story: I am a Scottish princess. My mother wanted me to get married and behave like a proper lady. But I had other plans, and didn't care about getting a husband. I love practicing archery or swordplay, riding my horse through the highlands. I love my freedom. A wicked witch transformed my mother into a bear for some time. But oddly, this whole adventure helped us understand each other more.

My message: Whatever it is they want you to be, you don't have to live according to *their* plans and rules. Even though they mean well. Your freedom has to speak first. You are who you are, and that is absolutely OK. Don't try to fit in, don't deny yourself, it can do no good. The path won't always be easy but it is the only one that can lead you to serenity. Trust my word, and do not try to conform to the wishes of others. Be your own and only ruler.

My story: I am the wild wolf standing before a full moon. I often appear in fairytales, though my appearance is feared most of the time. They say I'm cruel, hungry, and merciless. They say I eat little pigs, little boys, little girls, and grandmothers as well. They say I hide in the forest with my gleaming fangs and voracious appetite. But this is all a legend. I'm actually nobler, sweeter and more inspiring than what is said everywhere.

My message: I'm here to tell you that your inner wilderness needs to be heard and unleashed. Stop being reasonable, tidy, careful. Go through the forest, bay at the moon, dig your claws into the ground, and show your fangs. Run, growl, bark! The time has come to be wild. Your soul belongs to the night and moon. The wolf within you wants to be released, and act freely. So listen to this call, and unchain your inner wolf!

My story: At first I was scared and sad when I saw myself locked away in the castle of this ugly and frightful beast. But then I learned to open my heart. I taught my eyes to see beyond appearances. I discovered hidden beauty behind the beasty face. Therefore, I realized that a beast can be kind and gentle, and that true love can sometimes be born in the strangest of places.

My message: Do not trust what your eyes see, trust what your heart feels. Appearances can be deceiving. Maybe at first, things will seem dark and unpleasant. Give them a second thought, and don't make up your mind too hastily. Learn to open your heart. There is a great amount of beauty and love involved here, but they may be hidden from your sight for the moment. So close your eyes and trust your heart. You will discover wonders and treasures.

My story: The sultan Sharyar, having been hurt by a former unfaithful wife, resolved to marry a new girl each day, and have her killed the next day. When he married me, the daughter of the vizier, I started to tell him a tale. He wanted me to continue speaking the next night, and the night after, and the night after. And when 1001 nights had passed, the king, having fallen in love with me, decided to spare my life, and kept me as his inspired queen.

My message: What are the stories that live inside you and that you wish to tell? Offering the tales that fill your mind is quite important at this stage of your path. It could even save your life, in a symbolic way. So do not wait. Speak, write, compose, paint; whatever form you choose for your story, give it birth without delay. But remember: your audience needs to be captivated. So make your story unforgettable and addictive.

My story: I'm a nanny. But a very unusual one, you might say. I come down from the sky when children need me. I bring magic within my bag. When I appear, get ready to dance on rooftops, to be transported into drawings, or to learn unpronounceable nonsense words. But I also like discipline. I want things to be done efficiently and promptly. And when the wind changes, I must leave. But in the meantime, I fixed everything that needed fixing in the family I stayed with.

My message: Magic has to be mixed with discipline. Be creative, bring enchantment to this world, spread sparkles all around. But do not forget to incorporate a little etiquette and deportment. Order and method can do no harm to imagination. It's even the opposite. Magical creations can be magnified by some constraint. So stand up straight, tidy your room and fly high in the sky.

My story: I was my young master's only inheritance. At first, that despaired him. But soon he understood that I was no ordinary cat. I asked for a pair of boots, and promised him that I would make him rich. I built a whole plan: I told everyone that my master was the marquis de Carabas; I made him meet the king's daughter; and I defeated an ogre whose castle became my master's. He married the princess. Today he's rich and happy, and so am I.

My message: Your situation may not be bright at first sight. But don't get discouraged. Put on your boots and hat, and try to turn things to your advantage. Learn to fall on your feet like a cat. Make fire of any wood, use your cunning and your skills. Adapt to the situation and make the most of it. Maybe it will take some harmless shenanigans. That's no big deal. For in the meantime, it will lead you where you want to be.

27 · THE BLUE FAIRY

My story: There was this sweet man who wanted so badly to have a son. I granted his wish and gave him one, out of a wooden puppet. Pinocchio was the name of the puppet. I watched over him during his adventures, to get sure he grew wise. Then I transformed him into a real little boy. I only appear to those who have faith in my lucky star and gently pray for my intercession. If they're pure at heart, I grant their wish and pour magic in their lives.

My message: Rejoice and feel blessed. Your prayers have been heard, and your wishes are about to be granted. You have fought very hard to get where you are now, but the thing is: you've never lost hope, nor faith. Therefore you will be rewarded. This card really comes to you as a blessing and good omen. So just relax, celebrate and say thank you. Your dream is to come true very very soon.

My story: I was boring in grey Kansas with my little dog Toto. A twister dropped my house into the magical land of Oz. The good witch Glinda told me to follow the yellow brick road, to get to Emerald City, where the wizard lived. I met incredible people along the way. At the end of my adventures, I found out that I had the power to go back home just by clicking the heels of my magical ruby slippers, and also that home was, after all, the best place to be in.

My message: Sometimes you think you have to search far away what is just in your own backyard. Sometimes you have to be far away from home and far away from the ones you love to realize how much you love them all. Discover new lands, follow colored brick roads, meet interesting people, but keep in mind that your true home is always where your heart is. Home is your only real quest.

My story: Here I stand, at the end of the yellow brick road, in the magical land of Oz. Am I made of real emeralds? That is not the point, my dear. I am the place where the great wizard of Oz lives. I am the place where anything is possible. I am the place where Dorothy, the Scarecrow, the Tin Man and the Cowardly Lion got their rewards. I am the end of the quest, the time of celebration. I am the city of wonders, to be found beyond rainbows.

My message: The road was long and sometimes perilous. But look at yourself now! You have reached your goal, you have made your way to your Emerald City! This time should be one of celebration and reward! You ought to be proud of what you've done. You should rest a little and congratulate yourself. The adventure will go on for sure, but for now enjoy your achievements, for they are truly amazing.

My story: My father had this crazy plan of marrying me. I tried to discourage him by asking for incredible dresses, among which a dress as bright as the sun. As he could provide them, I asked for his magical gold producer donkey's skin. And when he provided it too, I escaped, disguised in this same donkey skin. Eventually, I found a prince; my father married another woman; I could shine again in my beautiful dresses; and everything went well at last.

My message: You have run away for too long, hiding yourself from the world, feeling ashamed and lonely, disguising your true feelings, your true face and your true beauty. There is nothing to fear anymore. You don't need to put on an ugly skin anymore. A time of radiance is beginning for you. Dare to show your true colors. Put on your brightest outfit and shine like a sun. Light fits you so well…

After your readings, make sure to store your deck in a safe place. If you want to re-energize your deck, place it upon a tales collection book for a whole night, and let the energy of the written lines infuse your deck.

DE LA NUIT ORACLE

L'Oracolo della Notte

C'ERA UNA VOLTA…

C'era una volta… una creativa coppia di artiste francesi, composta dalla talentuosa illustratrice Alexandra V. Bach e dall'esperta di Tarocchi Carole-Anne Eschenazi. Avendo già creato insieme i *Tarot De la Nuit* (I Tarocchi della Notte), hanno deciso di riunirsi di nuovo per esplorare il magico mondo delle fiabe. Carole-Anne ha selezionato 30 "personaggi" tratti da queste storie meravigliose, mentre Alexandra li ha interpretati attraverso la propria visione artistica. Così è nato il *De la Nuit Oracle* (l'Oracolo della Notte).

Volevano che questo mazzo fosse stimolante, magico e nello stesso tempo incantevole. Per il lettore, attraverso l'oracolo è possibile riconnettere sé stesso con il proprio bambino interiore, e lasciare che l'immaginazione che nasce dalle intuizioni più profonde del cuore possa prendere il comando, portando ad immergersi nella bellezza simbolica dei racconti e delle immagini. Cenerentola, Biancaneve, Peter Pan, Mary Poppins, Raperonzolo... sono nello stesso tempo personaggi e archetipi, pronti per diventare una guida per "vivere felici e contenti".

COME LEGGERE LE CARTE

Ci sono molti modi per leggere le carte. Il più semplice è sicuramente quello di pescare una singola carta. Il lettore deve concedere a sé stesso qualche minuto di calma per riflettere sull'immagine, sui personaggi, sulla storia – magari solo chiedendosi "cosa mi viene in mente?" grazie alle libere associazioni – e poi trasformare queste brevi riflessioni in qualcosa di utile nella propria giornata.

Potrebbe trattarsi di:

– un aspetto di sé da far emergere

– una situazione che si potrebbe presentare

– un'esperienza da cui trarre un insegnamento

– qualcosa che riguarda altri a cui prestare attenzione

Se si vogliono usare le carte in modo più diretto è possibile utilizzare metodi di lettura tradizionali, ad esempio quello chiamato "Le Favole della Notte".

METODO DELLE FAVOLE
DELLA NOTTE

Mescolare le carte e pescarne sette, posizionandole come nella figura.

1	2
3	4
5	6

7

1 – C'era una volta: rappresenta l'inizio della ricerca, il luogo da cui si parte.

2 – Debolezza: rappresenta una debolezza o una difficoltà, ciò che rende vulnerabili.

3 – Iniziazione: rappresenta l'avventura che si deve vivere per crescere e svilupparsi.

4 – Beneficio: rappresenta alleati e risorse su cui contare, che vengano da altri o da sé stessi.

5 – Magia: rappresenta ciò che si deve fare per portare più magia nella propria vita e nella situazione attuale.

6 – La Grande Lezione: rappresenta la lezione che si può imparare in questo momento.

7 – Felici e Contenti: rappresenta ciò che bisogna fare per ottenere un lieto fine.

LE CARTE DELLA NOTTE

Le descrizioni delle carte che seguono sono dei piccoli semi di ispirazione. Cercano di mostrare ogni carta da un punto di vista soggettivo. Questo perché, in primo luogo, ogni carta rappresenta un aspetto di ogni essere umano. Nel lettore, come in tutti noi, questi aspetti convivono, ciascuno di essi può essere più forte o più debole, magari portato in primo piano solo in certi momenti e situazioni. Alla fine, interpretare le carte non è "divinazione", nel senso di previsione del futuro, ma diventa un dialogo con sé stessi e con il mondo che ci circonda.

1 · LO SPIRITO DELLA MAGIA

La mia storia: credo nella magia, nelle fate e nei racconti. Devo solo far suonare il mio piccolo *carillon* e qualcosa di magico avviene. Non ho tempo da sprecare con quanti non ci credono, perché la magia è la fonte di tutto. Non smetterò mai di vederla ovunque e in ogni cosa.

Il mio messaggio: credi nelle fate e nella magia! Vedi piccoli miracoli ovunque. Connettiti con lo spirito della Grande Magia e lo vedrai all'opera nella tua vita. Credi nella magia e la magia crederà in te.

2 · ALICE NEL PAESE DELLE MERAVIGLIE

La mia storia: un giorno ho seguito un coniglio bianco nel Paese delle Meraviglie. Lì ho scoperto strani esseri e cose incredibili. Anche se era solo un sogno, è un viaggio di cui ne è valsa la pena.

Il mio messaggio: qualcosa ti chiama. Scoprirai un nuovo ambiente, che all'inizio probabilmente ti sembrerà confuso e al quale dovrai abituarti. Non lasciare, però, che questo ti fermi. Rimani aperta e curiosa, affamata di meraviglie. E sappi che il viaggio che ti aspetta è qualcosa che non dimenticherai mai.

3 · CENERENTOLA

La mia storia: ho vissuto con una matrigna odiosa e con le sue figlie cattive. Eppure, dentro di me, la speranza è rimasta intatta. Una notte, è apparsa la mia fata madrina per farmi andare al ballo nel quale ho trovato l'amore della mia vita.

Il mio messaggio: non lasciare che gli ostacoli ti buttino giù. Mantieni intatte la tua speranza e la tua bontà: allora i sogni diventeranno realtà. Presto riceverai un aiuto miracoloso. Fino ad allora, sii paziente e aspetta il momento in cui potrai brillare.

4 · BIANCANEVE

La mia storia: avevo una matrigna cattiva, gelosa della mia bellezza, che ha cercato di uccidermi con una mela avvelenata. I nani, di cui ero diventata amica, l'hanno sconfitta e io sono stata salvata.

Il mio messaggio: dimentica le persone invidiose e meschine che ti circondano. La gentilezza è una qualità essenziale. Fai del bene in questo mondo brutale. Alla fine il bene si dimostra più forte, quindi fai della gentilezza la tua bandiera.

5 · LA BELLA ADDORMENTATA

La mia storia: una strega malvagia mi ha predetto che mi sarei punta il dito su una conocchia e sarei morta. Per fortuna una fata buona ha modificato l'incantesimo e mi sono solo addormentata. Un bacio d'amore mi ha risvegliata.

Il mio messaggio: la pazienza e il riposo sono necessari. Sei esausta e il tuo corpo ha bisogno di recuperare. Prenditi una pausa dalla tua routine quotidiana. Dormi, rigenerati. Tutto il resto può aspettare.

6 · CAPPUCCETTO ROSSO

La mia storia: mentre andavo a trovare la nonna, ho incontrato il lupo cattivo. Imprudentemente gli ho indicato la strada, così lui ha divorato la nonna e ha preso il suo posto nel letto. Questa è stata una bella lezione.

Il mio messaggio: attenzione, il pericolo è in agguato! Fai attenzione a quello che dici o che fai. Stai in guardia, e non fidarti alla leggera: il "lupo" davanti a te può avere doppi fini. Stai lontano da lui, e sii vigile sul sentiero che ti condurrà a casa.

7 · BABA YAGA

La mia storia: sono una strega russa, molto temuta. Vivo in questa casa che vedete. Ho potere su tutta la foresta, ma mi piace banchettare con la carne degli incauti. Incontrarmi non è qualcosa che si dimentica.

Il mio messaggio: una potente iniziazione ti aspetta. Sei nel mezzo di una foresta oscura, di fronte a una casa in cui vive una creatura terrificante. Avrai bisogno di tutto il tuo coraggio. Conoscerai le lacrime, il dubbio e la paura, ma scoprirai anche le tue forze e verità interiori. E tutto questo ti farà crescere.

8 · LA MOGLIE DI BARBABLÙ

La mia storia: se avessi saputo cosa mi aspettava quando ho sposato questo signore... Mi aveva proibito di aprire questa stanza del castello, ma quando ci sono entrata, armata di una chiave d'oro, ho scoperto i cadaveri insanguinati delle sue precedenti mogli. Mi ha minacciato, ma i miei fratelli lo hanno fermato per sempre. E ora ci godiamo la sua fortuna!

Il mio messaggio: fai attenzione. Qualcosa di malvagio è all'opera e il tuo avversario è nascosto. Scopri la verità, per quanto sgradevole possa essere. Quindi raduna i tuoi alleati per sconfiggere questo nemico.

9 · LA REGINA CATTIVA

La mia storia: ero la più bella del regno, finché il mio specchio non mi ha parlato di Biancaneve! La gelosia mi ha consumato e ho escogitato un piano malvagio per liberarmi di lei. Impossibile!

Il mio messaggio: qui regnano la gelosia e la competizione. Che questa gelosia sia dentro o attorno a te, stai molto attenta, perché può portare al caos. Puoi vincere solo uscendo da questa rivalità.

10 · JACK E LA PIANTA DI FAGIOLI

La mia storia: ho scambiato la mia mucca per dei fagioli magici. Hanno fatto nascere un albero gigante che mi ha portato in una terra dove viveva un gigante tanto ricco quanto malvagio. Ho rubato il suo tesoro, in modo che io e la mamma potessimo vivere felici e contenti.

Il mio messaggio: non avere paura! Dimentica i tuoi recenti errori, sali sull'albero e vai a scoprire nuove terre dove ti aspettano fortuna e fama. Con la tua astuzia, sarai in grado di sconfiggere tutti i nemici.

11 · VASSILISSA LA BELLA

La mia storia: la mia crudele matrigna mi ha mandato da Baba Yaga a cercare il fuoco. Una bambola magica mi ha aiutato a fare ciò che la strega voleva. Sono tornata a casa con un teschio in fiamme come guida, il quale ha consumato la mia matrigna. In seguito, ho sposato lo zar.

Il mio messaggio: sii coraggiosa, alcune prove ti aspettano. Ma non temere, perché sarai aiutata. Continua pazientemente per la tua strada e potrai iniziare un nuovo capitolo della tua vita.

12 · HANSEL E GRETEL

La nostra storia: persi nella foresta, siamo arrivati davanti alla casa di pan di zenzero della strega. Ci ha imprigionato e ci ha fatto ingrassare per mangiarci. Ma noi siamo stati più astuti e siamo riusciti a buttare lei nel forno.

Il nostro messaggio: astuzia e solidarietà sono la chiave! Nelle situazioni più pericolose bisogna essere intelligenti, ma anche avere un buon partner. C'è forza nel numero. È meglio essere in due che da soli.

13 · L'INCANTESIMO OSCURO

La mia storia: appaio in tutti i racconti. Sono la maledizione lanciata sul cammino dell'eroe. Tuttavia, io non sono fatto per essere eterno. Grazie a me, l'eroe impara molto sulle proprie forze e risorse interiori, poi mi lascia alle spalle.

Il mio messaggio: fai attenzione quando concedi la tua fiducia. Ci sono ostacoli che devono essere superati. Raccogli le tue forze, e attraversa nebbia ed oscurità.

14 · LA PRINCIPESSA SUL PISELLO

La mia storia: un principe voleva sposare solo una vera principessa. Quando arrivai al suo castello in una notte di tempesta, per mettermi alla prova hanno messo un pisello nel mio letto, sotto 20 materassi. Al mattino, la mia delicata schiena da principessa era piena di dolori, e il principe mi ha sposato.

Il mio messaggio: fai come il mio principe e pretendi il meglio. Devi sapere cosa vuoi e perché lo vuoi. Non scendere a compromessi con i tuoi sogni, quindi continua a non accontentarti.

15 · LA PRINCIPESSA
E IL RANOCCHIO

La mia storia: una rana mi aiutò a recuperare una palla d'oro dal giardino in cambio di una promessa di matrimonio, che mio padre mi obbligò a mantenere. Inorridita, ho lanciato la rana contro il muro della mia stanza, ma il ranocchio è diventato un bel principe!

Il mio messaggio: hai dato la tua parola, devi mantenere la tua promessa. Non puoi sottrarti alle tue responsabilità. La situazione ti può sembrare sgradevole, ma c'è un dono nascosto. Lo scoprirai solo impegnandoti e mantenendo la tua parola.

16 · PETER PAN

La mia storia: vivo sull'"Isola che non c'è" con Campanellino e i Ragazzi Perduti. Ho giurato di non crescere mai. Combatto contro Capitan Uncino e a volte vado a Londra a trovare Wendy. Un po' di polvere magica e pensieri felici la fanno volare via con me.

Il mio messaggio: riconnettiti con il tuo bambino interiore, lontano dal mondo delle persone adulte. Dimentica le tue responsabilità per un po'. Quali sono i pensieri felici che ti fanno volare via? Cosa ti dice il tuo bambino interiore?

17 · LA SIRENETTA

La mia storia: lui era un principe, io una sirena: era un amore impossibile. Ho fatto un patto con una strega e ho ottenuto gambe umane, ma il principe ha scelto un'altra. Avevo sacrificato così tanto per lui! Mi ha spezzato il cuore.

Il mio messaggio: la situazione non è sana, sei tu a fare tutti gli sforzi e i sacrifici. Il tuo cuore è puro, ma non puoi accettare una situazione così ingiusta. Lascia queste acque torbide e trova invece un oceano più sano.

18 · RAPERONZOLO

La mia storia: una strega mi ha rinchiuso in questa torre, e usava i miei lunghi capelli per scalarla. Un giorno, un principe si è innamorato di me. Per rabbia, la strega ha tagliato i miei capelli e accecato il mio amore. Malgrado questo, alla fine lui mi ha trovato e ci siamo sposati.

Il mio messaggio: nella tua torre d'avorio hai imparato l'autosufficienza e la solitudine, ma ora devi trovare il mondo esterno. Il tempo vola. Scegli attentamente chi far entrare nel tuo mondo, ma soprattutto scegli di lasciare finalmente la tua "zona di conforto".

19 · MULAN

La mia storia: la guerra infuriava. Non potevo lasciare che mio padre, vecchio e stanco, andasse al fronte, così ho preso il suo posto, travestita da uomo. Con l'aiuto di un drago protettore, ho difeso l'onore del mio nome e della mia famiglia.

Il mio messaggio: forse non è questa la guerra che sei destinata a combattere, ma hai impegnato il tuo onore e devi difendere le persone che ami. Mettiti al riparo e armati di coraggio. Alla fine, sarai vittoriosa e tutti saranno orgogliosi di te.

20 · LA REGINA DELLE NEVI

La mia storia: annoiata nel mio palazzo di ghiaccio, ho rapito un ragazzo il cui cuore è stato congelato. Ma la sua amica Gerda è andata a cercarlo e lo ha salvato con le sue lacrime. Eccomi di nuovo sola...

Il mio messaggio: esci dal tuo isolamento. Lascia il tuo castello di ghiaccio. Fai nuove amicizie. Questo inverno deve finire e la primavera deve tornare. La neve è bella, ma non scalda il cuore.

21 · MERIDA

La mia storia: sono una principessa scozzese. Mia madre voleva che fossi saggia e che mi sposassi: io avevo altri piani. Una strega l'ha trasformata in un orso per un po' di tempo. Stranamente, dopo questa avventura siamo riuscite a capirci meglio.

Il mio messaggio: non scendere a compromessi con la tua libertà. È questa che conta, non quello che altri decidono per te. Non negare te stessa cercando di conformarti ai desideri della gente. Vivi solo secondo le tue regole.

22 · IL LUPO

La mia storia: sono il lupo selvaggio che ulula alla luna piena. I racconti mi descrivono come un implacabile assassino, ma questa è una leggenda. In realtà, sono una creatura nobile e gentile, che vive in armonia con la natura.

Il mio messaggio: la tua parte selvaggia ha bisogno di essere ascoltata. Ulula alla luna, corri nei boschi, mostra le tue zanne, smetti di essere prudente e sii selvaggio. Libera il tuo lupo interiore. La tua anima appartiene alla luna, alla notte e alla foresta. Libera quest'anima indomabile!

23 · LA BELLA (E LA BESTIA)

La mia storia: rinchiusa nel castello della Bestia, all'inizio avevo paura. Poi, andando oltre le apparenze, ho aperto il mio cuore e ho scoperto la sua bellezza nascosta. Così è nato un grande amore.

Il mio messaggio: le apparenze ingannano. Non credere a quello che vedono i tuoi occhi, credi a quello che sente il tuo cuore. Anche se la situazione ti sembra oscura e difficile, riconosci la bellezza e i tesori che può contenere.

24 · SHEHERAZADE

La mia storia: il sultano aveva deciso di prendere una nuova moglie ogni giorno e di ucciderla il mattino dopo. Quando mi ha sposato, ho iniziato a raccontargli storie meravigliose, per ben mille e una notte. Alla fine mi ha tenuto come sua regina.

Il mio messaggio: hai dentro di te qualcosa da dire che puoi comunicare al mondo. Potrebbe anche salvarti, simbolicamente. Quindi racconta le tue "storie", in qualsiasi forma esse siano, e assicurati di catturare il tuo pubblico.

25 · MARY POPPINS

La mia storia: sono una tata straordinaria che scende dal cielo e porta magia, ma anche una certa disciplina. Quando cambia il vento, è tempo che io vada. Nel frattempo, però, ho sistemato molte cose nelle case di coloro che mi hanno accolto.

Il mio messaggio: combina la magia con la disciplina. Sii creativa, ma costante. L'ordine e il metodo spesso alimentano l'immaginazione, non la limitano. Quindi stai dritta, metti in ordine la tua stanza e vola alto nel cielo.

26 · IL GATTO CON GLI STIVALI

La mia storia: sono l'unica eredità che il mio giovane padrone ha ricevuto. Dubbioso all'inizio, ha capito rapidamente che ero un gatto eccezionale. Con i miei stivali l'ho fatto sembrare un marchese, gli ho procurato il castello di un orco e gli ho permesso di sposare una principessa. Non male, eh?

Il mio messaggio: la situazione sembra difficile, ma "mettiti gli stivali" e volgi le cose a tuo vantaggio. Mescola un po' le carte, se devi, usa il tuo ingegno e la tua astuzia. Atterrerai in piedi come un gatto e raggiungerai i tuoi obiettivi.

27 · LA FATA TURCHINA

La mia storia: ho dato a Geppetto un figlio fatto da un burattino di legno. Ho vegliato su Pinocchio perché acquisisse saggezza e maturità, poi l'ho trasformato in un vero bambino. Appaio a coloro che credono nella mia stella ed esaudisco i loro desideri.

Il mio messaggio: rallegrati, i tuoi desideri stanno per diventare realtà. Hai lottato duramente e i tuoi sforzi saranno ricompensati. Appaio come un buon auspicio per dirti che stai per realizzare i tuoi sogni.

28 · DOROTHY GALE

La mia storia: mi annoiavo, in Kansas, finché un uragano non ha portato la mia casa nella terra di Oz. Consigliata dalla fata Glinda, ho seguito la strada di mattoni gialli verso la Città di Smeraldo.

Ho incontrato molti personaggi incredibili, e alla fine sono tornata a casa, battendo i tacchi delle mie scarpe magiche. Allora ho capito che "casa" era il posto migliore del mondo.

Il mio messaggio: a volte cerchi in lungo e in largo ciò che hai già a portata di mano. A volte, solo quando sei lontana da casa e da coloro che ami ti rendi conto di quanto sono importanti. Scopri posti meravigliosi, ma ricorda sempre qual è la tua vera "casa".

29 · LA CITTÀ DI SMERALDO

La mia storia: alla fine della strada di mattoni gialli, eccomi qui! Io sono il luogo dove vive il Mago di Oz: il luogo di tutta la magia, dove tutto è possibile. Appena oltre l'arcobaleno.

Il mio messaggio: brava! Hai raggiunto il tuo obiettivo e hai completato la tua ricerca. Ora è il momento di celebrare il tuo lavoro. L'avventura continuerà, ma, per ora, assapora e contempla le tue vittorie.

La mia storia: mio padre voleva sposarmi, e per conquistarmi mi regalò dei magnifici abiti. Ho dovuto fuggire, travestita con una pelle d'asino, creduta brutta da tutti. Alla fine, per fortuna, ha sposato un'altra donna e io ho sposato un principe!

Il mio messaggio: niente più fughe, niente più vergogna e niente più travestimenti. È arrivato il momento di brillare come il sole, mostrando il tuo vero volto e la tua grande bellezza. Non c'è più niente da temere: vai avanti in piena luce.

DE LA NUIT
ORACLE

El Oráculo de la Noche

Érase una vez... una creativa pareja de artistas francesas, formada por la talentosa ilustradora Alexandra V. Bach y por la experta en Tarot Carole-Anne Eschenazi. Habiendo creado ya juntas *Tarot De la Nuit* (El Tarot de la Noche), han decidido unirse de nuevo para explorar el mágico mundo de las fábulas. Carole-Anne ha seleccionado 30 «personajes» tomados de estas historias maravillosas, mientras que Alexandra los ha interpretado a través de su propia visión artística. Así nació *De la Nuit Oracle* (el Oráculo de la Noche).

Querían que esta baraja fuese estimulante, mágica y el mismo tiempo encantadora. Para el lector, a través del oráculo es posible volver a conectar con su niño interior, y dejar que la imaginación que nace de las intuiciones más profundas del corazón pueda tomar el mando, sumergiéndose en la belleza simbólica de las narraciones y de las imágenes. Cenicienta, Blancanieves, Peter Pan, Mary Poppins, Rapunzel... son al mismo tiempo personajes y arquetipos, listos para convertirse en una guía para «vivir felices y contentos».

CÓMO LEER LAS CARTAS

Hay muchas maneras de leer las cartas. La más sencilla es sin duda extraer una sola carta. El lector debe concederse a sí mismo unos minutos de calma para reflexionar sobre la imagen, sobre los personajes, sobre la historia - tal vez preguntándose «¿qué me viene a la mente?» gracias a las libres asociaciones- y después transformar estas breves reflexiones en algo útil en el propio día.

Podría tratarse de:

- un aspecto de sí mismo que sacar a la luz

- una situación que podría presentarse

- una experiencia de la que aprender una lección

- algo referente a los demás a lo que prestar atención

Si se quieren usar las cartas de modo más directo, es posible utilizar métodos de lectura tradicionales, por ejemplo el denominado «Las Fábulas de la Noche».

MÉTODO DE LAS FÁBULAS
DE LA NOCHE

Barajar las cartas y extraer siete, colocándolas como en la figura.

1 – Érase una vez: representa el comienzo de la búsqueda, el lugar del que se parte.

2 – Debilidad: representa una debilidad o una dificultad, lo que nos hace vulnerables.

3 – Iniciación: representa la aventura que debe vivirse para crecer y desarrollarse.

4 – Beneficio: representa a los aliados y los recursos con los que podemos contar, tanto si vienen de los demás como de nosotros mismos.

5 – Magia: representa lo que debe hacerse para aportar más magia a la propia vida y a la situación actual.

6 – La Gran Lección: representa la lección que se puede aprender en este momento.

7 – Felices y Contentos: representa lo que debe hacerse para llegar a un final feliz.

LAS CARTAS DE LA NOCHE

Las descripciones de las cartas siguientes son pequeñas semillas de inspiración. Intentan mostrar cada carta desde un punto de vista subjetivo. Se hace así porque, en primer lugar, cada carta representa un aspecto de cada ser humano. En el lector, como en todos nosotros, conviven estos aspectos, cada uno de estos puede ser más fuerte o más débil, tal vez visible en primer plano solo en determinados momentos y situaciones. Al final, interpretar las cartas no es «adivinación», en el sentido de previsión del futuro, sino que se convierte en un diálogo consigo mismo y con el mundo que nos rodea.

1 · EL ESPÍRITU DE LA MAGIA

Mi historia: creo en la magia, en las hadas y en los cuentos. Solo tengo que hacer sonar mi pequeño *carillón* y sucede algo mágico. No puedo perder el tiempo con los que no creen, porque la magia es la fuente de todo. Nunca dejaré de verla en todos los lugares y en todas las cosas.

Mi mensaje: ¡cree en las hadas y en la magia! Ve pequeños milagros en cualquier lugar. Conéctate con el espíritu de la Gran Magia y lo verás actuar en tu vida. Cree en la magia y la magia creerá en ti.

2 · ALICIA EN EL PAÍS DE LAS MARAVILLAS

Mi historia: un día seguí un conejo blanco en el País de las Maravillas. Allí descubrí seres extraños y cosas increíbles. Aunque no era más que un sueño, es un viaje que ha merecido la pena.

Mi mensaje: algo te llama. Descubrirás un nuevo ambiente, que al principio probablemente te parecerá confuso y al que deberás acostumbrarte. Pero no dejes que esto te detenga. Mantente abierta y curiosa, ansiosa de maravillas. Y recuerda que el viaje que te espera es algo que nunca olvidarás.

3 · CENICIENTA

Mi historia: he vivido con una madrastra odiosa y con sus hijas mezquinas. Sin embargo, la esperanza que albergaba en mi interior se mantuvo intacta. Una noche apareció mi hada madrina para llevarme al baile en el que encontraré al amor de mi vida.

Mi mensaje: no dejes que los obstáculos te desanimen. Mantén intactas tu esperanza y tu bondad: entonces los sueños se harán realidad. Pronto recibirás una ayuda milagrosa. Mientras tanto, sé paciente y espera el momento en el que podrás brillar.

4 · BLANCANIEVES

Mi historia: tenía una madrastra mala, celosa de mi belleza, que intentó matarme con una manzana envenenada. Los enanos, de los que me había hecho amiga, la derrotaron y me salvaron.

Mi mensaje: olvida a las personas envidiosas y mezquinas que te rodean. La amabilidad es una virtud fundamental. Haz el bien en este mundo cruel. Al final triunfa el bien, por eso sé un abanderado de la bondad.

5 · LA BELLA DURMIENTE

Mi historia: una bruja malvada predijo que me pincharía un dedo con el huso de una rueca y me moriría. Por suerte un hada buena modificó el encanto y solo me quedé dormida. Un beso de amor me despertó.

Mi mensaje: la paciencia y el descanso son necesarios. Estás agotada y tu cuerpo necesita recuperarse. Haz un descanso de tu rutina diaria. Duerme, regenérate. Todo lo demás puede esperar.

6 · CAPERUCITA ROJA

Mi historia: mientras iba a visitar a mi abuela, me encontré con el lobo malo. Cometí la imprudencia de indicarle el camino, de manera que devoró a la abuela y ocupó su lugar en la cama. Esta ha sido una gran lección.

Mi mensaje: ¡cuidado, el peligro está al acecho! Presta atención a lo que dices y a lo que haces. Mantente en guardia y no te fíes a la ligera: el «lobo» ante ti puede tener doble intención. Aléjate de él, y estate alerta en el camino que te llevará a casa.

7 · BABA YAGÁ

Mi historia: soy una bruja rusa, muy temida. Vivo en esta casa que veis. Tengo poder en todo el bosque, pero me gusta darme un festín con la carne de los incautos. Encontrarme es algo que no se olvida.

Mi mensaje: te espera una potente iniciación. Estás en el medio de un bosque oscuro, frente a una casa en la que vive una criatura terrorífica.

Deberás armarte de valor. Conocerás las lágrimas, la duda y el miedo, pero descubrirás también tus puntos fuertes y verdades interiores. Y todo esto te hará crecer.

8 · LA MUJER DE BARBA AZUL

Mi historia: si hubiera sabido lo que me esperaba cuando me casé con este señor... Me había prohibido abrir esta estancia del castillo, pero cuando entré, armada con una llave dorada, descubrí los cadáveres ensangrentados de sus anteriores mujeres. Me amenazó, pero mis hermanos lo detuvieron para siempre. ¡Y ahora disfrutamos de su fortuna!

Mi mensaje: ten cuidado. Algo malvado está al acecho y tu adversario está oculto. Descubre la verdad, por muy desagradable que sea. Después reúne a tus aliados para derrotar a este enemigo.

9 · LA REINA MALA

Mi historia: ¡era la más bella del reino, hasta que mi espejo me habló de Blancanieves! La envidia me consumía y urdí un plan malvado para deshacerme de ella. ¡Imposible!

Mi mensaje: aquí reinan la envidia y la competitividad. Presta mucha atención, tanto si la envidia está dentro de ti como a tu alrededor, porque puede sembrar el caos. Solo puedes ganar saliendo de esta rivalidad.

10 · JACK Y LAS HABICHUELAS MÁGICAS

Mi historia: cambié mi vaca por habichuelas mágicas. De estas habichuelas creció un árbol gigante que me llevó a una tierra donde vivía un gigante tan rico como malvado. Le robé su tesoro, para que mi madre y yo pudiésemos vivir felices y contentos.

Mi mensaje: ¡no tengas miedo! Olvida tus errores recientes, sube al árbol y descubre nuevas tierras donde te esperan fortuna y fama. Gracias a tu astucia, serás capaz de derrotar a tus enemigos.

11 · VASILISA LA BELLA

Mi historia: mi cruel madrastra me mandó a la guarida de Baba Yagá a buscar el fuego. Una muñeca mágica me ayudó a hacer lo que la bruja quería. Volví a casa con una calavera en llamas como guía, la cual consumió a mi madrastra. Después me casé con el zar.

Mi mensaje: sé valiente, te esperan algunas pruebas. Pero no tengas miedo, porque recibirás ayuda. Sigue con paciencia por tu camino y podrás comenzar un nuevo capítulo de tu vida.

12 · HANSEL Y GRETEL

Nuestra historia: perdidos en el bosque, llegamos delante de la casa de pan de jengibre de la bruja. Nos encerró y nos cebó para comernos. Pero nosotros fuimos más astutos y conseguimos meterla en el horno.

Nuestro mensaje: ¡la astucia y la solidaridad son la clave! En las situaciones más peligrosas es necesario ser inteligentes, pero también tener a un buen compañero. La unión hace la fuerza. Es mejor estar acompañados que solos.

13 · EL ENCANTO OSCURO

Mi historia: aparezco en todos los cuentos. Soy la maldición lanzada en el camino del héroe. Sin embargo, no me han creado para ser eterno. Gracias a mí, el héroe aprende mucho sobre sus fuerzas y recursos interiores, después me deja atrás.

Mi mensaje: presta atención en quién depositas tu confianza. Hay obstáculos que deben superarse. Ármate de valor y atraviesa la niebla y la oscuridad.

14 · LA PRINCESA Y EL GUISANTE

Mi historia: un príncipe solo quería casarse con una princesa de verdad. Cuando llegué a su castillo en una noche de tormenta, para ponerme a prueba pusieron un guisante en mi cama, bajo 20 colchones. Por la mañana, mi delicada espalda de princesa estaba muy dolorida, y el príncipe se casó conmigo.

Mi mensaje: haz como mi príncipe y elige lo mejor. Debes saber qué quieres y por qué lo quieres. No renuncies a tus sueños, así que sigue sin conformarte.

15 · LA PRINCESA Y LA RANA

Mi historia: una rana me ayudó a recuperar la pelota de oro del jardín a cambio de una promesa de matrimonio, que mi padre me obligó a mantener. Horrorizada, lancé la rana contra la pared de mi habitación, ¡pero la rana se convirtió en un bello príncipe!

Mi mensaje: has dado tu palabra, debes mantener tu promesa. No puedes eludir tus responsabilidades. La situación puede parecerte desagradable, pero hay una recompensa oculta. Solo la descubrirás comprometiéndote y manteniendo tu palabra.

16 · PETER PAN

Mi historia: vivo en el «País del Nunca Jamás» con Campanilla y los Niños Perdidos. Juré que nunca crecería. Lucho contra el Capitán Garfio y a veces voy a Londres a reunirme con Wendy. Unos polvos mágicos y pensamientos felices la hacen volar junto conmigo.

Mi mensaje: conéctate de nuevo con tu niño interior, lejos del mundo de las personas adultas.

Olvida tus responsabilidades por un momento. ¿Cuáles son los pensamientos felices que te hacen volar? ¿Qué te dice tu niño interior?

17 · LA SIRENITA

Mi historia: él era un príncipe, yo una sirena: era un amor imposible. Hice un pacto con una bruja y conseguí piernas humanas, pero el príncipe eligió a otra. ¡Había sacrificado tanto por él! Me rompió el corazón.

Mi mensaje: la situación no es sana, eres tú la que haces todos los esfuerzos y sacrificios. Tu corazón es puro, pero no puedes aceptar una situación tan injusta. Abandona estas aguas turbias y encuentra un océano más sano.

18 · RAPUNZEL

Mi historia: una bruja me encerró en esta torre, y usaba mi larga cabellera para escalarla. Un día, un príncipe se enamoró de mí. Por rabia, la bruja me cortó el pelo y cegó a mi amor. A pesar de esto, al final me encontró y nos casamos.

Mi mensaje: en tu torre de marfil has aprendido la autosuficiencia y la soledad, pero ahora debes encontrar el mundo exterior. El tiempo vuela. Elige bien a quién dejas entrar en tu mundo, pero sobre todo decide por fin abandonar tu «zona de confort».

19 · MULÁN

Mi historia: la guerra se enfurecía. No podía permitir que mi padre, viejo y cansado, fuese al frente, por lo que ocupé su lugar, disfrazada de hombre. Con la ayuda de un dragón protector, defendí el honor de mi nombre y de mi familia.

Mi mensaje: tal vez no sea esta la guerra que estás destinada a combatir, pero has comprometido tu honor y debes defender a las personas que amas. Protégete y ármate de valor. Al final, saldrás victoriosa y todos estarán orgullosos de ti.

20 · LA REINA DE LAS NIEVES

Mi historia: aburrida en mi palacio de hielo, rapté a un chico cuyo corazón se congeló. Pero su amiga Gerda fue a buscarlo y lo salvó con sus lágrimas. Y aquí estoy, otra vez sola...

Mi mensaje: sal de tu aislamiento. Deja tu castillo de hielo. Haz nuevas amistades. Este invierno debe terminar y la primavera debe regresar. La nieve es bonita, pero no reconforta el corazón.

21 · MÉRIDA

Mi historia: soy una princesa escocesa. Mi madre quería que fuese sabia y que me casase: yo tenía otros planes. Una bruja la transformó en un oso durante algún tiempo. Sorprendentemente, después de esta aventura nos entendimos mejor.

Mi mensaje: no renuncies a tu libertad. Esta es la que cuenta, no lo que lo que otros deciden por ti. No la niegues intentando adaptarte a los deseos de la gente. Vive solo según tus reglas.

22 · EL LOBO

Mi historia: soy el lobo salvaje que aúlla bajo la luna llena. Los cuentos me describen como un asesino implacable, pero esta es una leyenda. En realidad, soy una criatura noble y buena, que vive en armonía con la naturaleza.

Mi mensaje: debes escuchar tu parte salvaje. Aúlla a la luna, corre por el bosque, muestra tus colmillos, deja de ser prudente y sé salvaje. Libera tu lobo interior. Tu alma pertenece a la luna, a la noche y al bosque. ¡Libera esta alma indomable!

23 · LA BELLA (Y LA BESTIA)

Mi historia: estaba encerrada en el castillo de la Bestia y al principio tenía miedo. Después, dejando a un lado las apariencias, abrí mi corazón y descubrí su belleza oculta. Así nació un gran amor.

Mi mensaje: las apariencias engañan. No creas en lo que ven tus ojos, cree en lo que siente tu corazón. Aunque la situación te parezca oscura y difícil, reconoces la belleza y los tesoros que puede contener.

24 · SHEHERAZADE

Mi historia: el sultán había decidido coger una nueva mujer cada día y matarla a la mañana siguiente. Cuando se casó conmigo, empecé a contarle historias maravillosas, durante mil y una noches. Al final me conservó como su reina.

Mi mensaje: albergas en tu interior algo que decir que puedes comunicar al mundo. Podría incluso salvarte, simbólicamente hablando. Venga, cuenta tus «historias», de la forma que sea, y asegúrate de captar la atención de tu público.

25 · MARY POPPINS

Mi historia: soy una niñera extraordinaria que baja del cielo y aporta magia, pero también una cierta disciplina. Cuando cambia el viento, me tengo que ir. Sin embargo, mientras tanto he resuelto muchas cosas en las casas de aquellos que me han acogido.

Mi mensaje: combina la magia con la disciplina. Sé creativa, pero constante. El orden y el método suelen alimentar la imaginación, no la limitan.

Por ello debes ser disciplinada, ordena tu habitación y vuela alto en el cielo.

26 · EL GATO CON BOTAS

Mi historia: soy la única herencia que mi joven dueño ha recibido. Dudoso al principio, enseguida entendió que era un gato excepcional. Con mis botas le hice parecer un marqués, le conseguí el castillo de un ogro y le permití casarse con una princesa. No está mal, ¿verdad?

Mi mensaje: la situación parece difícil, pero «ponte las botas» y cambia las cosas a tu favor. Baraja un poco las cartas y, si es necesario, usa tu ingenio y tu astucia. Aterrizarás de pie como un gato y conseguirás tus objetivos.

27 · EL HADA AZUL

Mi historia: le di a Geppeto un hijo constituido por un títere de madera. Me preocupé de que Pinocho adquiriese sabiduría y madurez, después lo transformé en un niño de verdad. Me aparezco a aquellos que creen en mi estrella y cumplen sus deseos.

Mi mensaje: alégrate, tus deseos están a punto de hacerse realidad. Has luchado duro y tus esfuerzos serán recompensados. Aparezco como un buen augurio para decirte que estás a punto de realizar tus sueños.

28 · DOROTHY GALE

Mi historia: me aburría, en Kansas, hasta que un huracán se llevó mi casa a la Tierra de Oz. Aconsejada por el hada Glinda, seguí el camino de ladrillo amarillo hasta la Ciudad Esmeralda. Me encontré muchos personajes increíbles y al final volví a casa, chocando los tacones de mis zapatos mágicos. Entonces entendí que el «hogar» era el mejor lugar del mundo.

Mi mensaje: a veces buscas a tu alrededor lo que ya tienes a tu alcance. A veces, cuando estás lejos de casa y de aquellos que quieren te das cuentas de lo importantes que son. Descubre lugares maravillosos, pero recuerda siempre cuál es tu verdadera «casa».

29 · LA CIUDAD ESMERALDA

Mi historia: y al final del camino de ladrillos amarillos, ¡aquí estoy! Yo soy el lugar donde vive el Mago de Oz: el lugar de toda la magia, donde todo es posible. Justo al otro lado del arcoíris.

Mi mensaje: ¡enhorabuena! Has conseguido tu objetivo y has completado tu búsqueda. Ahora ha llegado el momento de celebrar tu trabajo. La aventura continuará pero, por ahora, saborea y contempla tus victorias.

Mi historia: mi padre quería casarse conmigo y, para conquistarme, me regaló bonitos vestidos. Tuve que escapar, disfrazada con una piel de asno, considerada fea por todos. Al final, por suerte, se casó con otra mujer y yo me casé con un príncipe.

Mi mensaje: se acabaron las huidas, la vergüenza y los disfraces. Ha llegado el momento de brillar como el sol, mostrando tu verdadera cara y tu gran belleza. No tienes nada que tener: sigue avanzando en plena luz.

DE LA NUIT
ORACLE

O Oráculo da Noite

ERA UMA VEZ...

Era uma vez... uma criativa dupla de artistas franceses, composta pela talentosa ilustradora Alexandra V. Bach e pela especialista de Tarô Carole-Anne Eschenazi. Tendo já criado em conjunto o *Tarot De la Nuit* (O Tarô da Noite), decidiram reunir-se novamente para explorar o mundo mágico das fábulas. Carole-Anne selecionou 30 "personagens" retiradas destas histórias maravilhosas, enquanto Alexandra as interpretou através da sua própria visão artística. Nasceu assim o *De la Nuit Oracle* (o Oráculo da Noite).

Pretendiam que este baralho fosse inspirador, mágico e ao mesmo tempo encantador. Do ponto de vista do leitor, o oráculo é uma possibilidade de contactar de novo com a sua criança interior e deixar que a imaginação que nasce das intuições mais profundas do coração possa assumir o controlo, levando-o a mergulhar na beleza simbólica das histórias e das imagens. Cinderela, Branca de Neve, Peter Pan, Mary Poppins, Rapunzel… são ao mesmo tempo personagens e arquétipos, prontos para se tornarem num guia sobre como "viver feliz para sempre".

COMO LER AS CARTAS

São muitas as formas de ler as cartas. A mais simples é certamente a de tirar uma única carta. O leitor deve reservar para si próprio alguns minutos de tranquilidade para refletir sobre a imagem, as personagens, a história — talvez se perguntando simplesmente "o que me vem à mente?" graças à livre associação — e depois transformar estas breves reflexões em algo útil para o seu dia.

Poderá ser:

– um aspeto de si mesmo a fazer emergir

– uma situação que poderá apresentar-se

– uma experiência da qual retirar uma aprendizagem

– algo relativo aos outros e sobre o qual estar atento

Se quiser usar as cartas de uma forma mais direta, é possível empregar métodos tradicionais de leitura, por exemplo, o chamado "As Fábulas da Noite".

MÉTODO DAS FÁBULAS DA NOITE

Baralhar as cartas e tirar sete, posicionando-as como na figura.

1	2
3	4
5	6

7

1 — Era uma vez: representa o início da busca, o lugar a partir do qual se parte.

2 — Fraqueza: representa uma fraqueza ou dificuldade, o que nos torna vulneráveis.

3 — Iniciação: representa a aventura que se deve viver para crescer e desenvolver.

4 — Benefício: representa aliados e recursos com os quais contar, sejam eles provenientes de outras pessoas ou de si mesmo.

5 — Magia: representa aquilo que é preciso fazer para trazer mais magia para a própria vida e para a situação atual.

6 — A Grande Lição: representa a lição que se pode aprender neste momento.

7 — Felizes e Contentes: representa o que é preciso fazer para se obter um final feliz.

AS CARTAS DA NOITE

As descrições das seguintes cartas são pequenas sementes de inspiração. Procuram mostrar cada carta de um ponto de vista subjetivo. Isto porque, em primeiro lugar, cada carta representa um aspeto de cada ser humano. No leitor, como em todos nós, estes aspetos convivem, podendo ser cada um deles mais forte ou mais fraco, e talvez só se revele em determinados momentos e situações. No fundo, interpretar as cartas não é "adivinhação", no sentido de prever o futuro, mas torna-se num diálogo consigo mesmo e com o mundo que nos rodeia.

1 · O ESPÍRITO DA MAGIA

A minha história: acredito na magia, nas fadas e nos contos. Basta-me apenas tocar no meu pequeno *carrilhão* para que algo mágico aconteça. Não tenho tempo a perder com quem não acredita, porque a magia é a fonte de tudo. Nunca deixarei de a ver em toda a parte e em tudo.

A minha mensagem: acredite nas fadas e na magia! Veja pequenos milagres em todos os lugares. Ligue-se ao espírito da Grande Magia e vê-lo-á em ação na sua vida. Acredite na magia e a magia acreditará em si.

2 · ALICE NO PAÍS DAS MARAVILHAS

A minha história: um dia segui um coelho branco até ao País das Maravilhas. Lá descobri estranhos seres e coisas incríveis. Mesmo que tenha sido apenas um sonho, é uma viagem que valeu a pena.

A minha mensagem: algo a chama. Descobrirá algo novo que provavelmente parecerá confuso ao início e ao qual terá de se acostumar. Não deixe que isso a impeça. Fique aberta e curiosa, ávida de coisas maravilhosas. E saiba que a viagem que a espera é algo que jamais irá esquecer.

3 · CINDERELA

A *minha história:* morava com uma madrasta odiosa e com as suas filhas malvadas. No entanto, dentro de mim, a esperança permaneceu intacta. Uma noite, a minha fada madrinha apareceu para me levar ao baile, no qual encontrei o amor da minha vida.

A minha mensagem: não deixe que os obstáculos a deitem abaixo. Mantenha intactas a sua esperança e bondade: os sonhos então tornar-se-ão realidade. Em breve receberá uma ajuda milagrosa. Até então, seja paciente e aguarde o momento em que poderá brilhar.

4 · BRANCA DE NEVE

A minha história: tinha uma madrasta malvada, com ciúmes da minha beleza e que tentou matar-me com uma maçã envenenada. Os anões, de quem me tinha tornado amiga, derrotaram-na e eu salvei-me.

A minha mensagem: esqueça as pessoas invejosas e mesquinhas em seu redor. A gentileza é uma qualidade essencial. Faça o bem neste mundo brutal. No fim, o bem prevalecerá, por isso faça da gentileza a sua bandeira.

5 · A BELA ADORMECIDA

A minha história: uma bruxa malvada previu que eu espetaria o dedo no fuso de uma roca e morreria. Felizmente, uma fada boa modificou o encantamento e simplesmente adormeci. Um beijo de amor despertou-me.

A minha mensagem: a paciência e o descanso são necessários. Está exausta e o seu corpo precisa de recuperar. Faça uma pausa na sua rotina diária. Durma, revigore-se. Tudo o resto pode esperar.

6 · CAPUCHINHO VERMELHO

A minha história: quando ia visitar a minha avó, encontrei o lobo mau. Imprudentemente, indiquei-lhe o caminho e por isso ele devorou a avó e tomou o seu lugar na cama. Esta foi uma bela lição.

A minha mensagem: atenção, o perigo está à espreita! Preste atenção ao que diz ou faz. Esteja alerta e não confie de ânimo leve: o "lobo" à sua frente pode ter intenções escondidas. Mantenha-se longe dele e fique vigilante ao longo do caminho que a levará para casa.

7 · BABA YAGA

A minha história: sou uma bruxa russa muito temida. Vivo nesta casa que vê. Tenho poder sobre toda a floresta, mas gosto de me banquetear com a carne dos incautos. Um encontro comigo não é algo que se esqueça.

A minha mensagem: aguarda-a uma poderosa iniciação. Está no meio de uma floresta escura, diante de uma casa em que vive uma criatura assustadora. Precisará de toda a sua coragem. Conhecerá as lágrimas, a dúvida e o medo, mas também descobrirá as suas forças e verdades interiores. E tudo isso a fará crescer.

8 · A MULHER DO BARBA AZUL

A minha história: se soubesse o que me esperava quando me casei com este senhor... Tinha-me proibido de abrir esta sala do castelo, mas, quando entrei nela, armada com uma chave de ouro, descobri os cadáveres ensanguentados das suas mulheres anteriores. Ameaçou-me, mas os meus irmãos pararam-no para sempre. E agora desfrutamos da sua fortuna!

A minha mensagem: tenha cuidado. Algo de malvado está em ação e o seu adversário está escondido. Descubra a verdade, por mais desagradável que possa ser. Em seguida, junte os seus aliados para derrotar este inimigo.

9 · A RAINHA MÁ

A minha história: eu era a mais bela do reino, até que o meu espelho me falou da Branca de Neve! Os ciúmes consumiam-me e eu elaborei um plano malvado para me livrar dela. Impossível!

A minha mensagem: aqui reinam o ciúme e a competição. Quer este ciúme esteja dentro de si ou em seu redor, tenha muito cuidado, pois pode levar ao caos. Só conseguirá vencer saindo desta rivalidade.

10 · JOÃO E O PÉ DE FEIJÃO

A minha história: troquei a minha vaca por feijões mágicos. Deles nasceu uma árvore gigante que me levou a uma terra onde vivia um gigante tão rico quanto malvado. Roubei o seu tesouro para que eu e a mamã pudéssemos viver felizes e contentes para sempre.

A minha mensagem: não tenha medo! Esqueça os seus erros recentes, suba a árvore e descubra novas terras onde a fortuna e a fama esperam por si. Com a sua astúcia, será capaz de derrotar todos os inimigos.

11 · VASILISA, A BELA

A minha história: a minha cruel madrasta enviou-me a casa de Baba Yaga para procurar fogo. Uma boneca mágica ajudou-me a fazer aquilo que a bruxa queria. Regressei a casa com uma caveira em chamas como guia, a qual consumiu a minha madrasta. Em seguida, casei-me com o czar.

A minha mensagem: seja corajosa, algumas provações a aguardam. Mas não tema, porque será ajudada. Continue pacientemente o seu caminho e conseguirá começar um novo capítulo da sua vida.

12 · HANSEL E GRETEL

A nossa história: perdidos na floresta, chegámos diante da casa de bolo de gengibre da bruxa. Aprisionou-nos e fez-nos engordar para nos comer. Mas fomos mais astutos e conseguimos metê-la no forno.

A nossa mensagem: a astúcia e a solidariedade são a chave! Nas situações mais perigosas, precisa de ser inteligente, mas também ter um bom parceiro. Há força no número. É melhor ser dois do que sozinho.

13 · O FEITIÇO DAS TREVAS

A minha história: apareço em todas as histórias. Sou a maldição lançada no caminho do herói. No entanto, não sirvo para ser eterno. Graças a mim, o herói aprende muito sobre as suas próprias forças e recursos internos e depois deixa-me para trás.

A minha mensagem: tenha cuidado quando confia. Existem obstáculos que precisam de ser superados. Reúna as suas forças e atravesse a névoa e a escuridão.

14 · A PRINCESA E A ERVILHA

A minha história: um príncipe só queria casar-se com uma princesa de verdade. Quando cheguei ao seu castelo numa noite de tempestade, puseram-me à prova colocando uma ervilha na minha cama por baixo de 20 colchões. De manhã, as minhas delicadas costas de princesa estavam muito doloridas e o príncipe casou-se comigo.

A minha mensagem: faça como o meu príncipe e procure o melhor. Precisa de saber o que quer e porque quer. Não faça concessões em relação aos seus sonhos, continue sem se conformar.

15 · A PRINCESA E O SAPO

A minha história: um sapo ajudou-me a recuperar uma bola de ouro do jardim em troca de uma promessa de casamento, que o meu pai me obrigou a cumprir. Horrorizada, lancei o sapo contra a parede do meu quarto, mas o sapo tornou-se num belo príncipe!

A minha mensagem: deu a sua palavra, precisa de manter a sua promessa. Não pode subtrair-se às suas responsabilidades. A situação pode parecer-lhe desagradável, mas há um dom oculto. Só o descobrirá comprometendo-se e mantendo a sua palavra.

16 · PETER PAN

A minha história: vivo na "ilha da Terra do Nunca" com Sininho e os Meninos Perdidos. Jurei nunca mais crescer. Luto com o Capitão Gancho e às vezes vou a Londres ver a Wendy. Um pouco de pó mágico e pensamentos felizes fazem-na voar para longe comigo.

A minha mensagem: ligue-se novamente à sua criança interior, longe do mundo dos adultos. Esqueça as suas responsabilidades por um bocado. Quais são os pensamentos felizes que o fazem voar para longe? O que lhe diz a sua criança interior?

17 · A PEQUENA SEREIA

A minha história: ele era um príncipe, eu era uma sereia: um amor impossível. Fiz um pacto com uma bruxa e ganhei pernas humanas, mas o príncipe escolheu outra. Tinha sacrificado tanto por ele! Partiu-me o coração.

A minha mensagem: a situação não é saudável e é você que faz todos os esforços e sacrifícios. O seu coração é puro, mas não pode aceitar uma situação tão injusta. Deixe estas águas turvas e encontre um oceano mais saudável.

18 · RAPUNZEL

A minha história: uma bruxa trancou-me nesta torre e usava os meus longos cabelos para a escalar. Um dia, um príncipe apaixonou-se por mim. De raiva, a bruxa cortou-me o cabelo e cegou aquele que eu amava. Apesar disso, ele acabou por me encontrar e casámo-nos.

A minha mensagem: na sua torre de marfim, aprendeu o que é a autossuficiência e a solidão, mas agora deve ir ao encontro do mundo exterior. O tempo voa. Escolha com cuidado quem quer deixar entrar no seu mundo, mas, acima de tudo, opte finalmente por sair da sua "zona de conforto".

19 · MULAN

A minha história: a guerra alastrava-se. Não podia deixar que o meu pai, velho e cansado, fosse para as linhas da frente, por isso tomei o seu lugar, disfarçada de homem. Com a ajuda de um dragão protetor, defendi a honra do meu nome e da minha família.

A minha mensagem: talvez esta não seja a guerra que está destinada a lutar, mas deu a sua palavra e deve defender as pessoas que ama. Proteja-se e arme-se com coragem. No final, sairá vitoriosa e todos ficarão orgulhosos de si.

20 · A RAINHA DAS NEVES

A minha história: entediada no meu palácio de gelo, sequestrei um rapaz cujo coração foi congelado. Mas a sua amiga Gerda foi procurá-lo e salvou-o com suas lágrimas. Eis-me de novo sozinha...

A minha mensagem: saia do seu isolamento. Deixe o seu castelo de gelo. Faça novas amizades. Este inverno deve terminar e a primavera deve regressar. A neve é bela, mas não aquece o coração.

21 · MÉRIDA

A minha história: sou uma princesa escocesa. A minha mãe queria que eu fosse sábia e me casasse: eu tinha outros planos. Uma bruxa transformou-a num urso durante algum tempo. Estranhamente, depois dessa aventura conseguimos entender-nos melhor.

A minha mensagem: não faça concessões em relação à sua liberdade. É ela que importa, não o que os outros decidem por si. Não se negue procurando conformar-se aos desejos dos outros. Viva apenas de acordo com as suas próprias regras.

22 · O LOBO

A minha história: sou o lobo selvagem que uiva durante a lua cheia. Os contos descrevem-me como um assassino implacável, mas isso é uma lenda. Na realidade, sou uma criatura nobre e gentil, que vive em harmonia com a natureza.

A minha mensagem: o seu lado selvagem precisa de ser ouvido. Uive para a lua, corra ao longo da floresta, mostre as suas garras, pare de ser prudente e seja selvagem. Liberte o seu lobo interior. A sua alma pertence à lua, à noite e à floresta. Liberte essa alma indomável!

23 · A BELA (E O MONSTRO)

A minha história: trancada no castelo do Monstro, a princípio tive medo. Depois, indo além das aparências, abri o meu coração e descobri a sua beleza oculta. Assim nasceu um grande amor.

A minha mensagem: as aparências enganam. Não acredite no que os seus olhos veem, acredite no que seu coração sente. Mesmo que a situação lhe pareça sombria e difícil, reconheça a beleza e os tesouros que ela pode conter.

24 · SHEHERAZADE

A minha história: o sultão havia decidido ter uma nova esposa todos os dias e matá-la na manhã seguinte. Quando se casou comigo, comecei a contar-lhe histórias maravilhosas, durante mil e uma noites. Acabou por me manter como a sua rainha.

A minha mensagem: tem algo dentro de si a dizer que pode comunicar ao mundo. Poderá também salvá-la, simbolicamente. Por isso, conte as suas "histórias", independentemente da forma que assumirem, e certifique-se de cativar o seu público.

25 · MARY POPPINS

A minha história: sou uma ama incrível que desce do céu e traz magia, mas também uma certa disciplina. Quando o vento muda, é hora de eu ir. Entretanto, pus em ordem muitas coisas nas casas daqueles que me acolheram.

A minha mensagem: combine a magia com a disciplina. Seja criativa, mas constante. A ordem e o método alimentam frequentemente a imaginação, não a limitam. Por isso, atenção à postura, ponha em ordem o seu quarto e voe alto no céu.

26 · O GATO DAS BOTAS

A minha história: sou a única herança que o meu jovem mestre recebeu. Com dúvidas a início, rapidamente percebeu que eu era um gato excecional. Nas minhas botas, fiz com que ele parecesse um marquês, consegui-lhe um castelo que pertencia a um ogre e que se casasse com uma princesa. Nada mal, hein?

A minha mensagem: a situação parece difícil, mas "enfie as botas" e vire as coisas a seu favor. Baralhe um pouco as cartas, se necessário, use o seu engenho e astúcia. Cairá de pés como um gato e alcançará os seus objetivos.

27 · A FADA AZUL

A minha história: dei a Gepeto um filho a partir de uma marionete de madeira. Vigiei Pinóquio para que adquirisse sabedoria e maturidade, depois transformei-o numa criança de verdade. Apareço aos que acreditam na minha estrela e realizo os seus desejos.

A minha mensagem: alegre-se, os seus desejos estão prestes a tornar-se realidade. Lutou arduamente e os seus esforços serão recompensados. Apareço como um bom presságio para lhe dizer que está prestes a realizar os seus sonhos.

28 · DOROTHY GALE

A minha história: entediava-me no Kansas até que um furacão levou a minha casa para a terra de Oz. Aconselhada pela fada Glinda, segui pela estrada de tijolos amarelos até à Cidade de Esmeralda. Conheci muitas personagens incríveis e, por fim, voltei para casa, batendo os saltos dos meus sapatos mágicos. Foi então que percebi que "casa" era o melhor lugar do mundo.

A minha mensagem: às vezes procura em toda parte o que está já ao seu alcance. Por vezes, só quando está longe de casa e daqueles que ama, é que se dá conta de como eles são importantes. Descubra lugares maravilhosos, mas lembre-se sempre de qual é a sua verdadeira "casa".

29 · A CIDADE DE ESMERALDA

A minha história: chegando ao fim da estrada de tijolos amarelos, aqui estou eu! Eu sou o lugar onde vive o Feiticeiro de Oz: o lugar de toda magia e onde tudo é possível. Logo depois do arco-íris.

A minha mensagem: boa! Alcançou o seu objetivo e terminou a sua busca. Agora é o momento de comemorar o seu trabalho. A aventura continuará, mas, por agora, saboreie e contemple as suas vitórias.

30 · A PRINCESA COM PELE DE BURRO

A minha história: o meu pai queria casar comigo e, para me conquistar, ofereceu-me magníficos vestidos. Tive de fugir disfarçada com uma pele de burro, considerada por todos horrível. Por sorte, acabou por se casar com outra mulher e eu com um príncipe!

A minha mensagem: sem mais fugas, sem mais vergonha e sem mais disfarces. Chegou o momento de brilhar como o Sol, mostrando o seu verdadeiro rosto e a sua grande beleza. Não há mais nada a temer: vá em frente em plena luz.

CAROLE-ANNE ESCHENAZI

Having studied literature and graduated from a cinema school in Paris, Carole-Anne Eschenazi is a french writer and a tarot expert. She is the author of several novels and tales, published in France and abroad. She has a passion for self-growth, spirituality, divinatory decks and fairy-tales. She is previously the author of the Cat Tarot and the Tarot de la Nuit, both available through Lo Scarabeo.

Facebook: CaroleAnneAuteur
Instagram: caroleanne_eschenazi

ALEXANDRA V. BACH

Alexandra V. Bach is a celebrated artist whose exceptional work has graced countless books covers in her native France. Her work is lush, mysterious and richly detailed, with a flare for fantasy and gothic romantic touch. She has also worked as CD cover artist for many bands worldwide, published three artbooks and has previously illustrated Le Tarot de la Nuit, available through Lo Scarabeo.

Facebook: alexandravbachofficial
Instagram: alexandravbach

FROM THE SAME AUTHORS:
TAROT DE LA NUIT

78 Tarot Cards and intruction booklet.

"Trois allumettes une à une allumées dans la nuit
La première pour voir ton visage tout entier
La seconde pour voir tes yeux
La dernière pour voir ta bouche
Et l'obscurité tout entière pour me rappeler tout cela
En te serrant dans mes bras."

– *Jacques Prévert*